THE MILLIONAIRES CODE

How one decision changed my life and the formula that made it possible

BY
JIM MATHERS

FOUNDERS OF THE MILLIONAIRES CLUB

Admiral Press

1315 Cleveland Street
Clearwater, FL 33755

Library of Congress Control # 1-15056456231

ISBN: 979-8-89397-927-5

Introduction

This is my story of how I became a millionaire.

But I can't tell you that part without first sharing how life **prepared me for it.** Because this isn't just a book. It's a story, **my story,** and like any real story worth telling, it has two parts.

The first part is messy. It's the part where I failed, struggled, and doubted everything. It's where I lost more than I thought I could handle. **It's where I hit rock bottom.** The second part is where everything started to change. Where I decided to make it, where I cracked the code, figured it out, and finally broke through.

Both parts matter. But I'd argue the first part is the most important. Because that's where the formula came from; the formula I'm going to share with you at the end of this book, a formula built from the ground up, shaped by real experience and hard-earned lessons, and a formula anyone can follow.

It wasn't easy putting all of this into words. It took a lot of courage to share my story—the raw, unfiltered parts I used to keep to myself. But I didn't write this to impress you. I wrote it for one reason: **to help you**.

Now, I won't pretend this book alone can change your life. It won't. But it *can* point you in the right direction. It *can* show you what's possible, give you a starting place, and maybe even light a small spark inside you.

But the rest? That's on you. At some point, you'll have to make a real decision—the kind that shifts your life. And when you do, you'll need to show up for yourself, again and again. You'll need to push through fear, failure, fatigue, and every reason to quit.

But if you do… If you keep going, no matter what, you'll look back one day and realize you made it. Not because you got lucky. But because you *decided* to.

So, if you're ready, come with me. Let me tell you **my story**, let me show you the steps I took, and maybe, just maybe, you'll find the ones you need to take too.

I believe in you. I really do.

Love,
Jim

Contents

Chapter 1
Rock Bottom

The Fall

I leaned back in my chair, exhaling slowly.

"How did I get here?"

"What in the world was I doing wrong?"

"I followed the rules."

"I worked hard."

"I kept my head down and stayed out of trouble."

I shook my head.

My thoughtful gaze landed on the degree in nuclear engineering that hung on my wall.

"That had to count for something, didn't it?" I thought to myself.

And yet, there I was.

Every day felt like a struggle.

I had no job.

The bills were stacking up.

And I had a quarter million dollars in debt breathing down my neck.

"It didn't make any sense!"

At first, I felt angry.

Then frustrated.

And then, I started doubting myself.

"Maybe I wasn't as smart as I thought."

"Maybe I wasn't meant to be successful."

"Maybe life had already decided where I was going to end up, and I was just playing along, pretending I had control."

I closed my eyes, squeezing them shut, trying to block out the overwhelming weight and pressure.

No matter how hard I worked, I was barely getting by.

To make things more challenging, my wife was pregnant with our first son, and the thought of being unable to provide for my family made my stomach twist.

I looked over at my wife.

She was sitting on the sofa, reading, unaware of the storm raging in my head.

She had complete trust in me, which only added to the pressure because, at that moment, **I wasn't sure I trusted myself.**

"How did I get here?"

"How did I let it get this far?" I asked myself.

I'd spent years in sales, **helping other people build their businesses,** making them tons of money, while I barely scraped by.

And now, I had nothing to show for it.

The hardest part of being fired wasn't that I lost my job.

I could always get another one.

It was that I'd been fired by my best friend!

I was still trying to make sense of it.

A person I trusted.

Someone I had worked with for almost a decade.

He looked me dead in the eye, emotionless, and said, *"Jim, you're fired. I don't need you anymore."*

Just like that, everything I had worked so hard to build was gone in the space of **one short conversation.**

That moment replayed in my head repeatedly.

All the years I had spent working, pushing, and proving myself.

The thousands of customers I had signed up by sharing my personal story. I had helped him grow his business and triple his income!

And in the end, none of it mattered because, I guess, as the owner, you can fire anyone you want, at any time!

The Silence at the Bottom

Lost in my thoughts, sitting in that heavy silence that only comes at rock bottom, I found myself weighing what I believed were my only two options.

I could play it safe.

I could swallow my pride, find another job, and keep working, hoping for the occasional raise, working as hard as possible to get by as I had done for so many years.

Or I could take a risk.

I could bet on myself and figure this thing out.

I could climb my way out of this hole I had dug myself into.

I thought about it.

I had taken the safe route my entire life.

I had always worked hard for someone else, and where had it gotten me?

And then it hit me!

I didn't have two choices, I had one!

Because at that moment, it became clear:

The only person I could truly depend on was myself.

Looking back, I wish I could tell you I had some kind of master plan worked out.

Some idea of how I would turn things around and rebuild my life, but I didn't!

On the contrary, I didn't have the slightest clue what to do.

All I knew was this:

I had to change something.

And I was the only person who was going to make that happen.

"But how?"

Reality hit me in the face.

I sank into my chair, my eyes unfocused, staring into nothing.

I realized I was truly at rock bottom.

And maybe admitting that to myself was a turning point, maybe when you've got nothing left to lose, you stop holding back?

Because in the middle of all the stress and uncertainty, with no direction in sight, I felt something.

A flicker of hope.

A thought.

A possibility.

And a quiet voice in the back of my mind whispered…

"Jim, you can figure this out. You always do."

Chapter 2
The Day my World Changed

A Trip into My Past

"You can figure it out. You always do."

I'd heard that before, countless times in fact.

It was what my mom used to tell my father whenever things got tough.

And somehow, he always did.

My father wasn't one to complain or make excuses.

He didn't take shortcuts or the easy way out.

And, although he never finished high school, **he was a genius.**

He could solve just about any problem we had.

We weren't rich, but we had what we needed, and we lacked nothing important.

Somehow, he made it all work.

Thinking about my father made me smile, and my eyes drifted to a photo of him near my desk.

There he was, mid-celebration, laughing, caught in a moment of pure joy.

I remembered exactly when that photo was taken.

Even with seventy to eighty-hour workweeks and five kids to provide for, my father always made the best of every situation.

"What would he say to me right now?" I thought.

The truth is, I didn't get to spend nearly as much time with him as I wish I had.

And the time we *did* have mattered more than I realized.

Whether I knew it then or not, he was always teaching me.

He taught me to work hard.

He showed me what it meant to keep going, no matter how rough things got.

But see, his lessons didn't come through words.

He wasn't one to sit there and lecture me.

Everything he taught me came through how he lived, how he carried himself, and how he handled every situation.

I leaned in toward the picture, as if it might somehow speak back.

And just like that, my mind slipped back to a time when I didn't have bills.

Didn't have debt.

Didn't carry the weight of the world on my shoulders.

Back to when I was 15 years old.

Back to the day when my life changed forever.

I didn't know it at the time, but a simple motorbike ride that day would become one of the most defining moments of my life.

The Best Ride of My Life

One hot summer day, my father promised my mom he'd finally paint our house.

Our house was over a hundred years old, weathered and stubborn, and as charming as it was, it felt like something *always* needed fixing.

Still, we were proud of it because it was our home.

As usual, I stayed behind to help my dad with the weekend project, while my mom took my brothers and sisters to Grandma Hazel's.

The heat was relentless.

By 8 a.m., our shirts had already begun to cling to us with sweat as we got started.

I scraped away the old, sun-hardened layers of paint while he followed behind, rolling a fresh coat over the wood.

The rhythm of it, the scrape, the roll, a grunt here, and a joke there, carried us steadily through the morning.

It was a little past noon, when my father stopped and said,

"Hey, Jimmy, let's take a break!"

I turned to him, and there it was, that mischievous smile I knew so well.

I didn't argue.

I climbed down from the ladder.

He held the garden hose as he drenched himself to cool off.

Without a word, he handed it to me, and I let the cold stream pour over my head.

We stood there for a minute, dripping, catching our breath.

He wiped the water from his face with the back of his hand, then looked at me.

"Hey, why don't you take my new motorcycle for a ride?" he said.

I froze.

His motorcycle?

It was a brand-new KZ 400, a powerful bike and nothing like the smaller one I rode every day on our dirt track.

I looked at it, gleaming under the afternoon sun as it sat in front of the porch.

It was heavy.

It was fast.

And I wasn't sure I could handle it.

I wanted to say no.

But I didn't.

Because my dad believed I could do it.

I looked at him, and he nodded, still wearing that same confident, mischievous smile.

"Sure," I replied, almost stuttering.

Swallowing my fear, I climbed on.

I turned the key, and the engine roared to life, a deep, growling sound that rattled through my chest.

It was mean, powerful… a little scary, but also kind of exciting.

At first, I was careful.

I eased onto our dirt track, keeping it steady.

The bike rumbled beneath me like it wanted to go faster.

I rode slowly and did my best to stay focused, but after a few minutes I started feeling cocky.

Maybe a little too cocky.

I picked up speed, trying to show off.

Trying to be cool, I flew around the corner, ready to stop right in front of my dad.

But as I approached him, I realized I was going a little too fast.

Panic kicked in, I squeezed the front brake harder than I should have, and BAM!

The bike slammed into the ground, and I went flying.

I hit the ground hard, but surprisingly, I didn't feel any pain.

All I could think about was how humiliating it was.

I scrambled to my feet, covered in dust.

The bike lay on its side behind me, engine still ticking.

I didn't dare look at my father yet.

I wanted to disappear, to rewind time, to erase the moment.

But he didn't yell.

He didn't even get mad.

He just walked over, helped me lift the bike, and said, *"Come over here. Let's talk."*

I dusted myself off as we sat on the porch.

Then he asked me, *"Do you know what being cool is?"*

I didn't answer.

Because at that moment, I knew I was anything but cool.

He nodded and said, *"Being cool is knowing what you're doing while you're doing it."*

It was a simple lesson, but the real lesson came in what he did next.

As if nothing had happened, he handed me a few dollars.

"Why don't you grab me a pack of cigarettes from the store, while I clean things up?"

Tom's general store was just up the road.

By the time I returned, he had put away the paint brushes and cleaned up the bike.

Then he pointed to it.

"Now, get back on."

I was shocked.

I had just crashed his brand-new KZ 400 and now he wanted me to ride it again.

I swallowed my fear and got back on.

The engine roared again, but this time, I wasn't shaken or swept up in the excitement.

I kept my focus.

I really paid attention to what I was doing.

I paid attention to how the bike handled on the dirt.

How it turned.

How the brakes responded.

And by the time I rode back to him, I parked it perfectly.

He nodded and smiled, giving me a pat on the back as I got off.

"Now that's being cool," he said.

A shiver ran down my spine.

I wasn't just cool, I felt proud, and I could tell my father did too.

"Okay, now hop on the back, let's ride to Grandma's house," he said.

My stomach dropped.

The highway?

I had never been on a motorcycle on the highway before.

As we cruised down the long, open stretch of asphalt, I held on so tightly to my dad that I was sure I would crush his ribs. But slowly, I started to relax.

I trusted him, and as the wind rushed past us at 90 miles an hour, I felt something I'd never felt before - the raw, electrifying freedom of the open road.

It wasn't just speed, it was a sense of weightlessness, of letting go, of being completely alive.

That ride was one of the best moments of my life.

The Night between Two Worlds

The whole family was already there when we arrived at Grandma's house for dinner.

It was a beautiful summer evening, one of those rare summer days in Mt Clemens, Michigan, where the sun was warm, the skies were clear, and everything felt right.

Before we sat down to dinner, my dad looked at me and said, *"Jimmy, why don't you take the bike down the road and see how it handles?"*

Grandma Hazel lived on a rough dirt road—gravel, potholes, ruts, the kind of road motorcycles don't normally like.

Although it would be tougher, I'd just learned my lesson, and this time, I was ready.

I took it slow, easing into each turn, steady on the throttle.

As my confidence grew, so did my speed.

Before I knew it, I was flying past Grandma's house at 80 miles an hour, whooping and laughing, the wind ripping past me.

Then, out of the corner of my eye, I saw my mom.

She had come outside, and she was furious.

She was standing there, yelling at my dad.

So, I slowed down, parked the bike, and ran over.

She wasn't mad at me.

She was mad at **him** for letting me ride the bike so fast on a dirt road.

I still remember what he told her.

"He's fine. I wouldn't have let him ride, if I didn't know he could handle it."

He then looked at me and winked as he whispered:

"You got this Jimmy. I know you do."

We went inside as the sun started to dip into the horizon, painting the sky in shades of gold and rose.

Dinner was simple, but perfect.

Grandma always had a way of making it special—big portions, rich flavors, and enough to feed an army.

We crowded around her old kitchen table, plates piled high, laughter bouncing off the walls.

After a long, hot day of work, it was the perfect ending.

But as perfect as it all seemed, I had no idea that night would change my life forever.

When it was time to leave, night had fully settled in.

The air was cool, the sky deep and quiet.

I grabbed my helmet and started to climb onto my dad's bike.

He said, *"No, it's too dark, I'll drive the bike home, you go home with Mom in the car."*

The five of us squeezed into the car with Mom, drove home, and I went to bed as soon as we got there, since we had to get up early for school.

I woke up the following morning to a quiet house.

I noticed both my parents weren't home, which was unusual.

It felt like something was off, but I got ready for school anyway.

Then, when I got there, the principal pulled me aside.

"Jim, you need to go home," he said, his eyes avoiding mine, fixed somewhere on the floor as he spoke.

Something was **definitely wrong**.

I ran all the way home, and when I walked through the front door, my whole world collapsed.

My mom stood there in tears and told me what had happened.

On the way home, my dad had been hit head-on.

And the person who hit him never stopped.

They left him in a ditch.

It didn't feel real.

How could someone so strong, so full of life, be gone in an instant?

I wrapped my arms around my mom, holding on as tightly as I could.

All I could think about was that last ride.

The way he had looked at me, with complete trust.

The quiet nod when he said, *"You got this, Jimmy."*

I had felt more connected to him than ever before.

And just like that, he was gone.

No warning.

No goodbye.

The warmth of what seemed to be a perfect evening the day before, was replaced by a hollow ache in my chest.

Nothing would ever be the same again.

At just fifteen, my father was gone from my life… **forever.**

My New Reality

It didn't take long for reality to set in.

My mom was now a single mother with five kids.

And even though I was only 15 years old, I knew one thing:

I had to step up.

I had to grow up.

It's what my father would have expected of me.

That meant getting serious about school.

That meant finding a job to help my mom support our family.

That meant taking responsibility for my younger siblings.

Because, the day my dad left us was the day my childhood ended.

I wasn't a kid anymore.

I quickly learned that the world didn't pause just because I had lost my father.

The next few years went by very fast.

I just kept moving forward, doing what had to be done.

Between school, my job, and helping my mom, there wasn't much time to think about the future.

But by the time I was 17, life took another unexpected twist.

As I neared the end of high school, my mom sat me down to tell me the truth.

I remember sitting at the kitchen table across from her.

Her hands were folded, and she looked serious.

"We don't have enough money for you to go to college," she said.

My father had worked his whole life, carefully putting money into not one but **two** insurance plans.

But with his passing so early, it wasn't enough—**not enough to send me to college and still keep our family afloat.**

I nodded, keeping my expression neutral.

But inside, it hit me like a ton of bricks.

I had always dreamed of going to the University of Michigan.

I wanted to be an engineer.

I wanted to understand things.

I wanted to know how the world worked!

I dreamed of creating something bigger than myself.

But my dreams wouldn't pay the tuition.

And just like that, I found myself at a familiar crossroads, stuck, uncertain, and trying to figure out my next move.

Chapter 3
All the Right Moves for the Wrong Life

Rerouting My Future

With University of Michigan out of reach, I had to find another way.

Trying to figure things out, I met with the school counselor who suggested I apply to one of the military academies that offered a full college education in exchange for five years of active duty after graduation.

He handed me a catalog filled with the different academies and the educational programs they offered.

As I looked through them, one thing immediately caught my attention—the Naval Academy in Annapolis, Maryland, offered a program in nuclear engineering!

To be honest, the Navy had never really crossed my mind before.

On one hand, it meant committing to five years of service after graduation.

But on the other hand, it offered a free top-tier education in engineering that I'd always dreamed of studying.

I took a few days to think things through, and the more I thought about it, I knew that it was the only option that made sense.

Yes, it was a huge commitment, but it was worth it because I could finally study engineering at a top-rated school.

I could finally figure out how this great big world worked and, most importantly, **where I fit into it.**

To make a long story short, I decided, applied, and got accepted.

And just like that, at 18 and fresh out of high school, I stepped into a whole new chapter of my life—The Naval Academy.

The Academy was no joke.

The discipline, the structure, the pressure.

The mental toughness required to survive.

It demanded everything from me.

But I pushed through, determined to succeed.

And, four years later, I stood at graduation with a degree in nuclear engineering in my hands.

I was proud.

But what mattered more than anything?

The way my mother looked at me.

She had traveled from Michigan to attend my graduation.

When I spotted her in the crowd, surrounded by my younger brothers and sisters, I saw her eyes filled with pride, her smile shining through the tears of joy.

I knew this moment wasn't just mine.

It was **ours.**

For the first time in years, she could finally breathe.

I had grown up.

I had made it.

And my mom knew I was going to be okay.

That weekend was one of the best I had ever spent with my family.

We celebrated, laughed, and reminisced about everything it took to get there.

And, for a moment, I let myself believe that life was finally falling into place.

A Realization in the Deep

But then, the part I hadn't really thought about began to set in—the reality of **being in the Navy**.

I had just graduated from two years of advanced nuclear submarine training.

It was May 1985, and there was no time to ease into life as a new Naval Officer.

The Cold War had escalated to one of its most dangerous peaks, and tensions remained high as the world watched a new Soviet leader, Mikhail Gorbachev, take the stage with uncertain intentions.

My orders were clear and more than a little intimidating.

I was to be stationed aboard a nuclear-powered submarine in the North Atlantic Ocean to hunt Russian ballistic missile submarines.

I'd chosen the Naval Academy because it offered a path to study engineering, a way to pursue something I was passionate about.

But now, holding my orders in hand, I realized I hadn't thought this far ahead.

This was real.

I wasn't just an engineer—I was a Naval Submarine Officer and a Nuclear Engineer, serving on active duty in the middle of the Cold War.

I was about to be responsible for safely operating one of the most advanced pieces of technology at the time— a nuclear-powered submarine.

And it wasn't just any nuke, it was the USS Flying Fish (SSN-673), one of the most advanced attack submarines of its time.

My thoughts swirled as the weight of it all slowly settled in.

"So, this is it," I thought to myself. *"I'm about to spend the next few years locked inside a steel tube, deep beneath freezing water… chasing Russian missile submarines."*

It was a little terrifying, but in the Navy, orders are orders, and so I packed up and within a few short days I was off to sea.

If you've ever seen the movie *The Hunt for Red October* with Sean Connery, that was my Naval experience.

For 3 months at a time, I lived in complete confinement, hundreds of feet below the ocean's surface, where the world above felt very far away.

And I'll tell you something about being on a nuclear submarine:

You learn what real pressure feels like.

It's not just the physical pressure of being deep underwater.

But mental pressure.

When you're in a steel tube under the ocean during the tense days of the Cold War, it's not just about you.

One mistake could mean the difference between life and death **for everyone aboard.**

I didn't get the luxury of "having a bad day."

I followed orders.

I had to stay sharp.

And, I became relentless.

Because that's what it takes to be part of a team where failure is not an option.

In those years, I lived through moments I will never forget.

Moments that pushed me to my limits.

Adrenaline-fueled missions.

Close calls that helped remind me just how **thin the line is between success and disaster.**

I forged memories and friendships that have stayed with me my entire life and helped shape how I see the world today.

But despite the value I found in those experiences, there was always a quiet thought lingering in the back of my mind.

Something I couldn't quite put into words, a feeling that was always there, just beneath the surface, waiting to be understood.

One night, after we had been submerged for what felt like forever, I was sitting at my station, staring at the glowing monitors, checking the nuclear reactor's readings like I had done a hundred times before.

No fresh air.

No sunshine.

No sense of time except for the clock on the wall, which could have been wrong, and I would have never known.

In the stillness of it all, surrounded by steel, silence, and softly humming machinery, it hit me:

Life wasn't about making the right choices or the wrong ones.

There were no perfect paths.

Life was just a series of chapters, each one unfolding into the next.

Every chapter brought its own lessons, its own challenges, something to carry forward.

And the key wasn't in trying to control the whole story but making the most of where I was, so I'd be ready for whatever came next.

Being a Naval Officer wasn't my full story; it was just another chapter in my life.

A chapter I needed.

Because down there, sealed inside a steel tube, deep beneath frozen water, I learned things no classroom could ever teach me.

I learned exactly what I needed to move forward.

But every chapter eventually ends, making space for the next one to be written.

And as that realization unfolded, that familiar feeling crept back in.

That quiet, persistent thought that there had to be something more.

Something beyond routines and responsibilities.

A deeper purpose.

A broader picture.

A bigger game.

A sort of inner drive to understand better, and to create something bigger than myself.

A curiosity that pushed me forward.

A need to keep growing, to keep searching.

And it was that feeling, that led to the next chapter in my life.

A chapter that, from the outside looking in would appear to be "success."

Was This "Success?"

After finishing my service in the Navy, I had what most people would consider a good life.

I had the title.

I had the degree.

I had the experience.

And I had what most of my friends at the time considered a "dream job."

A government consulting job.

It provided steady pay.

Great benefits.

A comfortable life.

I played golf on the weekends.

I had time off to spend with friends.

I had the money and freedom to visit my family back in Michigan.

On the surface, everything seemed perfect.

And for a moment, I thought… *"Ah, this is it. This is what success is supposed to feel like."*

At first, working as a government consultant felt fun, new suits, an office, and a calendar packed with meetings.

Unfortunately, after a few short months the excitement wore off.

The work was routine.

Predictable.

It lacked the intensity and sense of purpose I'd left the Navy to find.

And all too soon that quiet feeling crept back in: *"There's got to be more."*

I hung on, but as the months passed slower than molasses, I started asking myself.

"Is this it?"

"Is this really all there is?"

"Is this as good as it gets."

Middle-class life may have been stable… but it felt empty.

I'd wake up, go to work, come home, repeat.

There was no urgency, no tension, no challenge, and maybe that's what bothered me the most.

I started to question things, wondering where this was all going

And that's when—right in the middle of that quiet crisis—a good friend introduced me to an opportunity I never would've considered.

And my first reaction? *"Absolutely not!"*

Chapter 4
Breaking the Chains

The Eight-Year-Old Salesman

It was a Friday evening, and I was just leaving church when I heard my name.

"Jim!"

I turned to see my friend John waving me over.

I had been caught up thinking about my golf plans for the weekend, and his voice pulled me back into the present.

He stepped closer and said,

"Come work with me this weekend. I think you'd be perfect."

I laughed.

"Absolutely not!"

John worked as a door-to-door salesman on the weekends, and if there was one thing I swore I would never do, **it was sales.**

I had spent my entire life believing that salespeople were liars.

Because I had been one.

Not by choice but by circumstance.

See, I had my first—and what I thought would be my last—sales job when I was eight years old.

My school had set up a way for us to earn our spot at the Boy Scout's annual camping trip by selling these small tool kits.

It was supposed to be simple.

If you sold twenty, the trip was paid for.

And I **really** wanted to go!

Every day after school I went through my neighborhood, excitedly pitching all my neighbors, telling them the truth: that if they bought a toolkit from me, it would help me go to summer camp.

And it worked.

Just one day before the deadline, I sold my twentieth kit!

I was proud… until the night before I left.

As I finished packing, I noticed my dad opening one of the toolkits he'd bought to help me out.

He was trying to fix something in the kitchen when the screwdriver snapped clean in half the moment he used it.

My heart sank.

I spent two weeks convincing my entire neighborhood to buy a cheap toolkit that wouldn't even last through one use.

I felt terrible.

I felt ashamed.

At that moment, I decided that **all salesmen are liars.**

And I swore I would **never be a salesman.**

So, you can imagine my reaction when my friend John asked me to learn door-to-door sales to make some extra cash!

"Come on," insisted John.

"Just give it a shot. If it doesn't work out, what's the worst that can happen? You lose a weekend?"

He kept pushing.

Telling me how he saw something in me.

That I had the personality for it.

That I could be good at it.

I wasn't convinced but he was right; I had nothing to lose.

So, I agreed.

"Fine," I said. *"One weekend—that's it."*

The Old-New Car

That weekend, I drove to a *Burger King*, where I was told to meet the sales team and manager.

The second I stepped inside, I knew I had made a mistake.

It was a perfect day for golf.

And I was wasting it on this?

In the back of the *Burger King*, huddled around a table with half-eaten burgers and scattered fries, sat a group of guys—salesmen.

And they **looked** like salesmen.

Loud.

Cocky.

Seasoned.

You could tell by the way they talked, laughed, and leaned in like they were always about to close a deal.

One guy noticed me staring at them.

He took one look at me and said, *"You must be the new guy!"*

They all laughed.

I was dressed for golf.

"You can't sell in shorts," one of them shouted.

I was **this close** to turning around and walking out.

I even started walking toward the door when someone stopped me.

"Jim?"

"Are you Jim?" he repeated.

"Yeah," I said.

"Hi, I'm Bill," he said. *"I'll be showing you how this works."*

I shook his hand.

I was still skeptical but decided to go along with it.

After all, I had already given up my weekend and it was long past tee time.

He took about fifteen minutes to explain the sales pitch, and then we hit the streets.

Everyone had an assigned neighborhood.

We were selling discount cards for a local auto repair shop.

As it was my first day, I followed Bill, watching him do the first few sales.

As I listened to his pitch, I realized that this was a very good deal for the customer.

And, it seemed straight forward, all I had to do was knock, pitch who ever answered, and go to the next house.

I watched Bill close a few more customers, all in a row.

People were buying and they weren't even asking many questions.

When I saw that Bill had made more in half an hour than I made in an hour as a nuclear engineer, I started to get interested.

"Let me try." I asked.

He smirked,

"Nobody closes a deal on their first day."

I had been told the same thing by the guys at Burger King, the same guys who said it was impossible to sell in shorts.

"Challenge accepted!" I replied.

I grabbed the stack of coupons from his hands and before he realized it, I knocked on the door.

A 16-year-old kid answered.

It caught me off guard.

I almost asked for his dad, but then I remembered the rule:

Pitch whoever answers the door.

So, I dove in.

Before I could even finish, the kid cut me off.

"You see that car?" he said, pointing to an old Chevy in the driveway.

"That's my new car! And it needs a lot of work."

I looked at the car. It wasn't new, but it was new to him.

He disappeared inside and came back with forty bucks.

"I'll take two! One for me and one for my friend, he just got a new car too!"

Bill stood there, stunned.

"Nobody closes a deal on their first day. And definitely not a 'double'," he laughed.

As we walked to the next house, something clicked.

I felt good about that sale.

And the kid was happy.

He wanted it.

He needed it.

And I hadn't lied about anything.

It was nothing like my experience as an 8-year-old.

That day I sold at nearly every door I knocked on.

And by the end of the day, making five sales an hour, I'd earned more than twice what I made at my government consulting job.

I kept going the next few weekends, knocking on doors, making sales, having fun, and making great money.

Before I knew it, my weekend sales job was consistently bringing in more than double what my so-called "**successful**" consulting job was and so I quit and went all in on sales.

Naturally, my mom was disappointed.

I remember trying to explain it to her—and in doing so, I realized that to most people, I already had what looked like a great life.

I had an easy job.

A steady paycheck.

A respectable career.

But for whatever reason, **I didn't feel successful.**

Something was missing.

And while I didn't have all the answers yet, I knew one thing for certain:

Sales gave me something my government job never could.

It challenged me.

It pushed me.

It allowed me to connect with people, with purpose, with possibility.

It was more than a job; **it was my next chapter**.

A new space to learn, grow, and stretch beyond what I thought I could do.

And through it, I found a whole new platform to understand life a little better, through countless experiences and interactions.

A Plate of Warm Cookies

One of the most unforgettable experiences began with a sweet old lady and a plate of warm chocolate chip cookies.

It was the first door on my route that day.

An elderly woman answered, smiling.

I had moved on from the auto repair coupons and was selling discount coupons for a local dry-cleaning service.

The coupons could save you a decent amount of money, **if you did a lot of dry cleaning.**

I asked my usual question:

"How much dry cleaning do you do?"

The lady smiled and said, *"Oh, a lot!"*

I stood at her door, chatting a bit about her family, and I explained how the discounts worked.

"I'll take one," she said, reaching for her checkbook.

In that short conversation with her, I learned that her husband had passed, her kids had left home, and she lived alone.

I had a funny feeling that her definition of *"a lot,"* was different from mine.

Curious, I asked her, *"How much dry cleaning is a lot?"*

She laughed, and said she took her favorite blanket to the drycleaner once every four years.

I quickly did the math in my head.

At that rate it would take her one hundred years to use and benefit from the discount card. I couldn't do it. I couldn't sell it to her.

I shook my head and politely replied, *"Ma'am, as much as I would like to sell you a discount card you really don't do enough dry cleaning for this to be fair to you."*

She insisted.

I refused.

I could tell she wasn't really interested in what I was selling, she just wanted to be nice.

She'd been politely listening, telling me stories about her kids, and I realized, she just wanted a way to give something back.

So, I gave her an out.

When she first opened the door, the smell of freshly baked cookies hit me. So I smiled and asked, *"Do you have any cookies?"*

"Yes, I just baked some," she replied inviting me inside.

I sat down and she brought me a plate with three massive chocolate chip cookies and a glass of milk.

We chatted more about her family as I took the last few bites of her amazing cookies, and then I thanked her and headed out.

I smiled to myself as I walked to the next house, still thinking about our brief but kind exchange.

A minute later, I knocked on the next door.

A woman opened it and immediately said, *"I'll take two."*

I was confused; I hadn't even started my sales pitch yet.

She smiled and explained. *"Sandy from next door called me."*

I handed the lady two coupons and headed to the next house, shaking my head and laughing to myself at how funny the whole thing had been.

At the third door of the day, a man answered.

"I'll take a coupon," he said.

I looked at him, by then I had caught on.

"Did Sandy call you?" I asked, laughing in disbelief.

He smiled, held out a $20 bill, and said, *"Yep."*

That day, every single house on that block had received a call from Sandy, and every single person who answered their door bought from me.

That's when I learned the most important lesson in sales.

A lesson I still apply every day and teach to every salesperson I meet:

Never sell someone something they don't need.

It wasn't just good sales advice; it was a principle for life.

Because in the end, every door I knocked on, every story I listened to, and every conversation I had wasn't just about making a sale, it was about learning to understand people.

And with each experience, I was growing into a better version of myself.

Full Circle Back to Reality

Over time, I built a career in sales, and it was a promising one.

I learned more than I ever thought possible and made more money than I imagined I would.

By staying honest, applying what I'd learned, and genuinely connecting with people, I built a better life.

I got happily married and began to feel like I was settling down.

But it wasn't perfect.

Even though I was doing what I thought I was supposed to, checking the boxes, living a "normal" life, an undercurrent of restlessness persisted.

Like something was incomplete.

Pretty soon, that quiet voice returned—**there had to be something more.**

I had been here before, a stable job, a steady paycheck, a "good life." I was doing better than I'd ever done, and yet, it was as if every time I reached a new level, life gave me a quiet nudge, urging me to keep going.

To keep searching.

But things weren't getting any easier.

The challenges felt bigger.

The setbacks felt heavier.

And my responsibilities kept piling up.

I'd come a long way since knocking on doors in Washington, D.C.

My sales skills led me to Seattle, where I joined my best friend in managing his chiropractic clinic, bringing in new patients, growing the business, and building something we both believed in.

For a while, I felt like things were lining up.

I was part of something that mattered, working with someone I trusted.

But financially, I wasn't doing great.

What looked like success from the outside was just a façade.

Behind the scenes, I was carrying debt, my paycheck barely covered the bills, and I was constantly struggling just to keep up.

So, I did the only thing I knew how to do, I kept showing up, I kept my head down, and I stayed focused. But I never stopped long enough to ask where it was all actually going.

I had worked hard my whole life, followed the rules, doing everything I thought was right.

And yet, somehow, I still found myself asking the same questions:

"Is this really it?"

"Is this all there is?"

Something was missing.

Something was off.

And that's when I made the decision.

A decision that would change my life forever.

A decision that would completely reshape my journey.

A decision that would open the next chapter of my life—a chapter that, in its own way and before I even realized it, would shift the entire course of my life *again!*

Chapter 5
The Decision

Leading Up to My Decision

It was July 1998, and my wife and I were down in Florida taking a short break from the grind.

That's when I bumped into an old friend, Mike, who asked me what appeared to be a normal question:

"So, Jim how are you doing?"

Without missing a beat, I gave my usual answer, *"I'm doing great!"*

It came out so easily, so automatic, like muscle memory.

Something I had said a thousand times before.

But Mike didn't just nod and move on.

He knew me.

Really knew me.

So, he looked me in the eye, and asked again.

"How are you really doing?"

This time, his question hit me like a ton of bricks.

I opened my mouth, but no words came out.

Instead, something inside me cracked open.

Before I even knew what was happening, I started crying, uncontrollably.

Years of stress, exhaustion, frustration, all of it poured out of me.

I wasn't doing great.

I wasn't even okay.

I had been telling myself I was fine because I didn't want to face the truth.

But in that moment, there was no hiding from it.

I had to change something.

I looked at my life, really looked at it.

I had been working overtime, I was stressed, and I was helping someone else build **their** business, while I was barely getting by.

The debts were piling up and the pressure of trying to keep my head above water was overwhelming.

No matter how hard I worked, I couldn't seem to break free from this hamster wheel of a life.

It was a lot to process.

A few days later, I really started to confront my life up to that point, and what I needed to do to change it.

All my life, I had kept pushing forward, but something inside me was always restless.

It was the same feeling I had in the submarine.

The same feeling that pushed me to leave my "successful" government consulting job.

The same feeling that had surfaced time and time again over the years.

There had to be more to Life.

But I had never figured out what it was.

I had tasted tidbits of success along the way.

However, I understood that personal success was not enough for me and that being financially free was only one step in the right direction.

I grew up in a small town in Michigan, poor but with a loving family.

Life was simple.

But I was a curious boy.

I was always searching.

I studied engineering because I wanted to understand life, how things worked, why things happened, and ultimately, I tried to figure out where I fit in.

By really confronting my life, my situation, and my true purpose, I realized:

Personal success, the kind of life I and many others were chasing, **was only one piece of the puzzle.**

I realized there were millions out there, each with their own dreams, their own struggles, and their own battles to fight.

All the people I met when I worked in sales, knocked on doors, and the countless conversations I had, were leading me to this moment.

I felt a surge of responsibility for everyone around me, and a strange sense of responsibility for the people I hadn't even met yet.

Every interaction, every handshake, every story I heard, opened my eyes a little more.

Being honest.

Doing the right thing.

Helping people.

That was life.

And that's when my goal completely shifted.

Just like that, the answer to the question I had been asking myself for years finally came into focus, clear, undeniable, and right in front of me:

I wanted to be successful so I could help others.

I wanted to make a difference in people's lives.

Because real success and happiness, I realized, wasn't just about what I could achieve.

It was about what I could give.

It was about how I could make others feel.

Life wasn't just about me!

Yes, I wanted financial freedom for myself and my family.

Of course, I wanted to live better, be happier, and provide for the people I loved.

But deep down, what really drove me wasn't just my own personal success.

It was the desire to help others achieve success.

To help others break free, achieve financial freedom, and live the life they dreamed of.

It sounded noble.

It sounded right.

But reality hit me.

I, personally, wasn't anywhere near financial freedom.

On the contrary, I was barely getting by.

And I remember thinking to myself…

"How am I supposed to help others if I'm drowning?"

Between everything that was happening in my life, the debt, the stress, and the feeling of running in place and going nowhere, **my new goal felt like a fantasy.**

A storm of thoughts swirled in my head, memories of where I had been, the weight of where I was now, and the fading outline of the dream I was barely holding onto.

I took a deep breath and exhaled slowly, shaking my head.

"I have to change something," I thought to myself.

But doubt crept in, its voice quiet, whispering:

"It's impossible."

"You're not good enough."

"Life is stacked against you."

I could barely keep my own world afloat, let alone chase something bigger.

I shook my head again.

My past and current failures loomed over me, and my fears told me to keep my head down, play it safe, and avoid the risk of failing again, like I had done my entire life.

Another failure would be too much to handle.

I sat there, lost in thought.

And then, out of nowhere, something powerful happened.

The thousands of thoughts and worries consuming my mind were silenced.

It was strange.

But my mind felt clear for the first time in a long time.

And in that moment of complete clarity, I made a decision:

"By the time I was 40—just two years from now—I would make my first million dollars."

The Million-Dollar Decision

For some reason, the moment I made that decision, I just knew I would make it.

A quiet certainty settled over me.

It seemed crazy.

It was crazy.

I wasn't making anywhere near that kind of money.

And I had **no plan on how I would do it.**

But for whatever reason, on that day and at that time, I knew I would make it.

I had to make it happen.

I had no choice.

No matter what it took, no matter how many obstacles stood in my way, I would make my first million dollars by the time I was 40.

I grabbed a blank piece of paper, and without even thinking, I wrote it down:

$1,000,000

I circled it twice.

It felt amazing.

I smiled and then started laughing.

Just making the decision, writing it down, seeing it in front of me, deciding it was possible, somehow lifted my spirits.

It gave me a newfound sense of purpose.

It wasn't just about the money; it was about what it represented.

Yes, making money would relieve the crushing financial stress that had been weighing me down, but more importantly, it would give me the freedom, time, and opportunity to focus on what I now knew truly mattered to me.

Helping others.

Unfortunately… that's not the end of my story.

See, deciding to make a million dollars is very different from making it.

Yes, without that powerful decision, I would have never made it.

But, despite my excitement, things didn't quite fall into place right after my decision.

On the contrary…

Things got worse.

Because the very next day, was the day I was fired by my best friend in Seattle.

I couldn't believe it.

I thought to myself, what am I going to do?

I had just made the decision to become financially free and immediately after it, I lost my job.

Now… imagine how hard that hit me?

I had to support my family, keep up with my payments, and suddenly, I had no job and no income.

Everything I had been worried about suddenly felt twice as heavy.

Life was mocking me.

I had every reason to give up my dream at that moment.

I had every reason to tell myself, *"I'll never make it,"* or *"This is a sign from God to just give up."*

I had every reason to go back to the way I had always done things, to just work, as an employee, and do the best I could.

But something about my decision kept me steady, like an anchor in the storm.

Because deep down, I knew the truth:

That if I wanted to make a million dollars, if I was going to help others, **I couldn't do it working for someone else.**

I had to start my own business.

It was the only way forward.

The only way I would ever create real financial freedom.

But despite knowing that, I had been holding myself back.

For some reason, I didn't fully trust myself.

I doubted my ability.

I didn't know where to start, and the risk of it all loomed over me like a giant question mark.

The unknown was terrifying, and every doubt I had ever felt about myself seemed to come rushing back at once.

"What if I failed?"

"What if I made things worse instead of better?"

I had been I clinging to the one thing I understood—the security of a steady paycheck.

Even if it wasn't enough to pay **all** the bills.

Even if it kept me stuck in life.

It was predictable. It was safe.

Looking back, losing my job turned out to be a blessing in disguise, though it didn't feel like that at the time.

Hitting rock bottom gave me an unexpected sense of clarity.

In a strange way, the lowest point in my life revealed exactly where I was meant to go.

But that didn't change the reality in front of me—**I was still at rock bottom.**

I had no money. And no clue where to even begin with starting a business.

I had set my goal: I had two years to make my first million.

But my first priority?

Keeping the lights on.

Keeping up with the bills flying at my face, while I figured out how to make it happen.

Luckily, I got a job opportunity in Virginia at a consulting company. It was all the way across the country, but I thought maybe a fresh start in a new state would help me rebuild faster.

I packed up everything I had and drove across America in my old, beat-up Honda with so many miles on it that it practically ran on hope instead of gas.

When I got there, I moved into a small room in the back of a friend's house and started the job.

Amazingly, within three weeks of working there, my wife, Fu-Mei, told me she was pregnant with our first son, Seamus.

That changed everything.

Suddenly, my responsibilities were bigger than ever before.

And then, less than a week after finding out I was going to be a father—I was fired again.

Two jobs. One month. Fired both times.

I was crushed, again.

I had debts to pay. A wife to support. And now, a child on the way. There was no time to feel sorry for myself. I had to do something.

Determined to succeed, I didn't waste any time.

Within three days, I landed another job—this time as a sales manager for an energy company in Florida.

So, once again, I packed up everything we owned and moved to Florida. It was our second long-distance move in just 4 weeks.

This time, we settled into a tiny room with a twin bed and a small closet we stuffed with the clothes we wore daily.

We lived simply, watching every dollar, knowing that now, more than ever, every decision mattered.

I had no background in energy sales, but I knew how to sell.

I quickly learned the business and worked as hard as I could.

But there was something different this time.

With my newfound purpose, **to become financially free and help others do the same,** driving me forward, something interesting happened.

I started doing really well.

I was helping sales reps become super successful, and at the same time, I was breaking sales records for the company.

Not long after I took over, the numbers shot up, the company performed better, and I wasn't just "getting by."

For the first time in a long time—**I was getting ahead.**

I was making more money than ever before.

I started paying down bills.

I had extra cash to spend.

Life became comfortable again.

Within three short months, I bought a new car, moved to a nicer apartment, and I was once again "successful."

But I hadn't forgotten my goal.

No amount of success in this job would change the fact that I wasn't where I truly wanted to be.

I knew I had to start my own business.

And as it turned out, my quick success as an energy sales manager opened the door to that exact opportunity.

One day after learning every aspect of the energy sales business, I was approached by an investor who, seeing how well I was doing as the sales manager, was willing to provide the capital for me to start my own energy company.

My instant reaction was hesitation.

It felt risky.

I had finally rebuilt my life—was I really ready to take a leap and change course?

Running my own company?

That was uncharted territory.

A massive responsibility.

The "old" me, who kept his head down, focused on paying the bills, and stuck to what was safe, wanted to say no.

But I quickly caught myself.

That wasn't me anymore.

I had made a powerful decision.

I had a powerful purpose.

I was going to make a million dollars, and then, I was going to help others do the same.

And now, here was my chance—**staring me right in the face.**

See, we all get chances like this in life.

Sometimes, multiple times.

But those chances are riddled with self-doubt, fear of failure, and many reasons to say no.

In the end, it all comes down to a choice.

And I had already made mine.

So, no matter how scary it seemed.

No matter how much my fears and doubts tried to creep in.

No matter the risk of walking away from a respectable and stable paycheck.

And no matter how uncomfortable it felt.

I went all in.

I started my own energy sales company.

I had no clients.

No safety net.

No guarantee of success.

But I had learned the basics of the business, and I had to trust myself.

Climbing Without a Safety Net

The first step was finding a client—an energy supplier we could sell for.

I was excited, but I had no illusions.

I knew this wasn't going to be easy.

And I was right.

The early days were grueling.

With nothing but a phone, a fax machine, and sheer determination, I dove in headfirst.

I worked 12 to 14-hour days, calling potential energy suppliers, faxing decision makers, and trying to get anyone—anyone—to take a chance on me.

The rejections came fast and hard.

Most wouldn't even give me the time of day.

Others strung me along for weeks before disappearing without a word.

I was exhausted and frustrated.

And with every unanswered call and every failed attempt, doubt crept in.

Was this a mistake?

Had I overestimated myself?

Had I walked away from comfort and stability again to end up right back where I started?

But whenever those thoughts tried to pull me down, I reminded myself of my decision.

I made a promise to myself.

And I wasn't about to break it.

So, despite the frustration, I kept going.

It finally happened after three straight weeks of talking to every supplier under the sun, moon, and stars— endless calls, pitches, and endless rejections.

Then, a supplier actually said **yes**.

I couldn't believe it at first.

I almost thought I had misheard them.

But no.

It was real.

I had done it!

I hung up the phone, sat back in my chair, **and just breathed.**

Relief.

Excitement.

A rush of adrenaline.

This wasn't just a deal - it was validation of all my efforts.

It was proof that I wasn't crazy for taking this risk.

All the long nights, the unanswered calls, and the rejections hadn't been for nothing.

I had cracked open the door.

And now, it was time to kick it wide open.

Without wasting a second, I got to work.

I rushed to Office Depot and bought every phone they had in stock.

I rented a small office space, threw in some tables and chairs, put together a sales script, hired a team, and got to work.

No more waiting.

No more hoping.

We were in business.

And almost immediately, the deals started rolling in.

We were making sales, and signing contracts.

Things were going great.

I could feel the momentum shifting in my favor.

"Ah, I made it!"

I thought all my hard work had finally paid off.

But life has a way of pulling the rug out from under you when you least expect it, and I never saw this one coming.

We had been making consistent sales for two weeks, and everything was running smoothly.

Then, at the start of the third week, I was expecting our first payment, and an email landed in my inbox.

Instead of a payment notification, I found a cold, impersonal message informing me that our contract was terminated, effective immediately.

No explanation.

No discussion.

And to make it worse, they weren't paying the invoices we sent.

The sales we made and the deals we had closed over those two weeks, were all for nothing.

At first, I thought there had to be some mistake.

I picked up the phone, called my contact at the company, and contested it.

But there was no way around it.

I was running a small sales operation—just 10 guys in a rented office space, making calls and closing deals.

They were a billion-dollar energy supplier.

I had no leverage.

No way to fight back.

And just like that, everything I had worked for over the last month vanished.

On top of my own personal worries, I now had an entire team depending on me.

Payroll was due, the business bills had to be paid, and the money I had counted on was nowhere to be found.

This wasn't how it was supposed to go.

We had done everything right.

We had made the sales, followed the process, and delivered exactly as promised.

And yet, in one ruthless email, it was all wiped away.

This feeling felt familiar.

I'd been here before.

I took a deep breath, trying to think through my next move.

I still had my investor's backing - for now.

But how long would that last if I couldn't turn things around?

I had to find another supplier. Fast.

Hanging by a Thread

I've been called stubborn before—sometimes for the right reasons, sometimes for the wrong ones.

But this time?

It was with good reason.

I refused to let one setback define me.

I wasn't about to give up now—not when I had come this far.

So, I did the only thing I knew how to do.

I picked up the phone.

Call after call.

Rejection after rejection.

Each "no" felt heavier than the last, pressing down on me, testing me.

But I kept going.

Then, finally, I got another yes!

Our second client.

Call it luck.

Call it persistence.

Call it whatever you want.

All I knew was that we were back in the game.

Without wasting a second, I got to work.

I hired more people, refined our sales script, and hit the ground running.

We started selling again.

And for a moment, it felt like we were on solid ground.

I thought we made it.

But life had other plans.

After another two weeks, the exact same thing happened.

My second client dropped me and wouldn't pay.

At that point, it felt like the world was telling me to give up.

I was two months in and had nothing to show for it.

In just two months, I had lost $70,000 of my investor's money, and I thought he was going to kill me.

Twice, I had built something.

Twice, it had been ripped away.

And if I was being honest with myself, I didn't know how many more hits I could take.

Doubt crept in, sinking its claws into my mind.

"Maybe, I wasn't cut out for this."

"Maybe, this was a mistake."

"Maybe, I should just take the loss and move on to a normal job."

Fear whispered every worst-case scenario in my ear.

I had a family to support.

I wasn't some reckless 20-year-old with nothing to lose.

That night, I had a conversation with my wife.

She knew some of what was happening—but not everything.

I had kept the worst of it to myself, carrying the weight alone, not wanting to worry her.

But as we talked, I saw something in her eyes.

She trusted me.

She believed in me.

And if she did, **then I had to believe in myself.**

I thought back to that moment at my desk—the day I made the decision that set this all in motion.

That wasn't just some dream.

That wasn't just a number on a piece of paper.

It was a commitment.

It was how I could feel at peace with myself.

It was the key to finding my place in the world.

It was how I was going to be able to help other people.

So, I did the only thing I could do.

I took a deep breath.

I pushed all my doubts aside.

And I picked up the phone.

Again.

One Last Attempt

By now, I knew the game—calls, faxes, rejections.

I had learned how to handle common concerns, reach the right people, and refined my pitch.

Finding my third supplier came a little easier.

And just like that, I was off again.

A third time.

I hired more people, got things moving, and we started making sales.

But as the end of that second week approached, I started to wonder what would happen.

I had been here before.

Twice.

And I simply couldn't afford another setback.

I did my best to stay positive, but I couldn't help but think about it.

"What if this was just another repeat?"

"Another unpaid invoice?"

"Another false start?"

Then, the third week arrived.

I held my breath as I checked for the payment.

And this time—it came!

Not only did my supplier pay me, but they were so impressed with our work that they asked me to hire even more people to keep up with demand.

I kept going.

I scaled the sales team from 10 to 100 people.

And soon enough, we reached a point where we were making over **500 sales a day.**

A few months into record-breaking sales, I got a call from my supplier.

"Jim, we need to talk."

There was something in his voice—an urgency I hadn't heard before.

"We can't keep up," he said. *"You need to shut it down."*

I was shocked, but this time was different, I had momentum.

Within a few days I found a new supplier and kept the team selling just as if nothing had happened.

My company grew and grew.

Each small victory stacked on top of the last, fueling my confidence and pushing me forward.

It wasn't overnight.

It wasn't easy.

And it certainly wasn't without more setbacks.

The months that followed were a whirlwind.

The deals kept coming.

The sales kept climbing.

And for the first time in my life, I wasn't just surviving.

I was thriving.

Then, one month before my 40th birthday, I reached the milestone I had been chasing.

I made $1,000,000 profit by the time I turned 40!

I sat back in my chair, staring at the figure, almost not believing it.

After everything, the failures, doubts, and fear of not being good enough, I did it.

It was as if everything I had been through in life, the good times and the bad times, all led up to this moment.

Relief flooded me, followed by something I hadn't felt in a long time.

I was proud of myself!

Not because of the money I had made, but because of what it represented.

It meant that all the sacrifices, all the sleepless nights, and all the times I had chosen to keep going instead of giving up—had all been worth it.

I thought back to the day I sat at my desk, drowning in debt, circling that number on a piece of paper.

Back then, that goal felt so far away.

But here I was.

I made it.

And, just as I promised myself, I spent the next two decades doing exactly what I had set out to do.

I traveled the world.

I spoke to rooms full of thousands of people—entrepreneurs, dreamers, and those standing at the same crossroads I had once faced.

I shared my story not because I had all the answers but because I knew what it felt like to struggle, doubt yourself, and wonder if success was really possible.

I wanted to show people that their **dreams ARE possible.**

And I knew that if I, a poor kid from a small town in Michigan, could find true success, then **so could anyone.**

It became my mission in life.

Helping others break through.

Guiding them through the same fears and doubts that once held me back.

Showing them that success lies just beyond their comfort zone.

Watching them take control of their lives and build something of their own.

And all the while, the energy sales business I had built from the ground up kept growing—far beyond what I had ever imagined—giving me the financial freedom to pursue my dream fully.

But through all of it.

Through the highs, the lows, and the lessons learned.

There was one question that kept coming up.

What did I learn from all of this?

Chapter 6
Cracking the Code

It Started with A Million Dollar Question

The stage lights were blinding.

The energy in the room was electric.

I stood before thousands of business owners, entrepreneurs, and dreamers, speaking at a major event overseas.

By that point, it had been several years since I started speaking on stage, sharing my experiences, and helping others break through their barriers.

But that day would begin a new chapter in my life.

As I stood there, looking out at the sea of faces, I asked a simple question: *"Who wants to become a millionaire?"*

The reaction was immediate.

The room exploded in cheers.

People jumped to their feet.

Hands shot into the air.

The energy was overwhelming.

I had spoken at hundreds of events.

I had helped thousands of people.

But at that moment, on that stage, it suddenly dawned on me.

This was what I needed to do.

Not just inspire people.

Not just tell my story.

Not just teach business strategies.

I needed to help people **become millionaires.**

I needed to show them that if I could do it—so could they.

It wasn't about luck.

It wasn't about being in the right place at the right time.

There was a process.

There was a way to do it.

There was a way for anyone to become a millionaire, even from rock bottom!

And all I needed to do was teach them what I did.

If they followed the same steps I took, they could achieve the same success.

It was that simple.

But then, a question I had never thought to ask myself...

How exactly did I do it?

I knew I had made it.

I knew I had climbed out of debt and overcome failure and the impossible.

I had built a business from scratch and made millions.

But I had never stopped to analyze **how**.

What had I actually done?

What were the exact steps that took me from rock bottom to millionaire?

Steps that I could easily explain to someone else.

Teach someone.

Guide someone through.

For the first time in a while, I had to turn the spotlight back on myself.

Because if I was going to help others do the same, I needed to understand my own success inside and out.

I had to figure out what I did and how I did it - down to a science.

Reverse Engineering Success

Finally, it was time to put my nuclear engineering degree to good use!

After that event, I flew home, and for the next few months, I was determined to figure it out.

I was determined to crack the code of **how to become a millionaire.**

I spent hours every day analyzing my journey.

I looked back at every moment of struggle.

Every time, I thought I wouldn't make it.

The mountain of debt.

The setbacks.

The failures.

The pressure.

I looked at what kept me going.

The persistence that pushed me forward.

The breakthroughs that fueled my momentum.

The determination that refused to let me quit.

The resilience that carried me through the worst days.

The small victories that reminded me of why I started.

And the fire inside me that never burned out—no matter how many times life tried to put it out.

And I kept asking myself…

What did I do?

It certainly wasn't luck.

It wasn't being in the right place at the right time.

I didn't win the lottery.

I didn't inherit money from a long-lost rich uncle.

So, what was it?

What did I do that took me from total disaster to complete success?

I had to figure it out!

Because if I could figure it out.

If I could distill what I did in exact steps, **I could teach it to anyone.**

I could create a system.

A blueprint.

A roadmap that others could follow.

After months of breaking it all down, dissecting every move I made, and asking myself the tough questions…

I finally cracked the code—**the millionaire's code.**

I discovered the ten exact steps that took me from rock bottom to millionaire.

These weren't just theories or motivational soundbites.

These weren't just ideas or abstract concepts.

They were real, tangible actions—things I had done in the precise order I had done them. This was my formula.

And it was clear enough that I could teach it.

Simple enough that anyone willing to put in the work could follow it.

I couldn't guarantee that everyone who followed these steps would become a millionaire—because challenges will always exist.

And after all, success isn't something I could hand to them.

It would always come down to the person—their commitment, their resilience, their purpose, their willingness to push forward no matter what.

But what I could give them was a precise blueprint.

A proven system that worked.

Building the Blueprint

Now, I could have just said,

"Here are the ten things I did to become a millionaire…"

I could have laid them out step-by-step, and called it a day.

I could have kept speaking on stage, sharing my story, and telling people how I did it.

I could have put the ten steps in a booklet and made them available.

But knowing how I did it isn't the same as doing it.

So, if I genuinely wanted to help people.

If I wanted to make a difference.

If I wanted to change people's lives—**I needed more!**

Because now that I had cracked the code for myself, I had to figure out something just as challenging…

How could I get others to do the same—no matter their circumstances?

And how could I help thousands - not just a select few?

So, the answer was simple.

I needed more than just a course or a program.

I needed to build a community!

A place where like-minded people could come together, support each other, and grow.

A place, where success wasn't just an individual pursuit but a shared journey.

And a place where I could provide mentorship, education, motivation, and inspiration to help people achieve their own dreams and goals.

So, I created *The Millionaire's Club.*

The Millionaire's Club became my mission.

My purpose.

My way to ultimately fulfill my own dream. And as I worked with people, guiding them through this process, I realized something…

There was one step that made all the difference.

One step that was more important than all the others.

Because without it, none of the other steps would have mattered.

It was the first step I took to become a millionaire.

It is the first step anyone needs to take to achieve success.

A step so simple that many overlook it.

A step so fundamental that some discount it.

Yet, it's the first and most powerful step!

Because without this step, success would remain just an idea.

A wish.

A "someday" that never comes.

But when you take this first step…

You may not fully realize its impact.

You won't see the complete picture right away.

You won't know exactly where it will lead.

But if you do it right and commit to it, and if you hang on and keep going no matter the challenges that get thrown your way—and there will be challenges—it becomes the spark that sets everything in motion.

And it will take you exactly where you want to go.

Chapter 7
The First Step of The
Millionaire's Code

The Power of Decision

Have you ever stopped and really thought about the power of your decisions?

Every day, your mind is flooded with thoughts. And every day, you make decisions, some small, some big.

Maybe today, you decided what to eat for lunch.

Maybe tomorrow, you'll decide something that changes the entire course of your life.

The life you are living right now is the direct result of the decisions you've made.

Some decisions are easy.

Others feel impossible.

And sometimes, you make a decision because you feel like you have no other choice. Because you're backed into a corner. Because it's the only path forward that makes sense **at that moment.**

Other times, you have multiple choices laid out in front of you, each leading in a different direction, and you have to decide which one to take.

But one thing remains true:

Your life—right now—is a reflection of the choices you've made.

Every success.

Every failure.

Every opportunity you took, or passed up.

Your career.

Your relationships.

And yes, even your financial situation.

I know this might be hard to accept because there are times when you feel like you have no other choice.

Sometimes, you feel stuck in a job, a relationship, or a financial situation.

Maybe it feels like the odds are stacked against you, like success just wasn't meant for you.

Trust me, I've been there. I've felt all of that and more.

I wasn't born into success, and life certainly didn't make it easy for me. But I made it.

And in doing so, I came to a true but undeniable realization:

Everything about your life today is a result of the decisions you made yesterday, last month, last year, or even decades ago.

And the craziest part?

Most of those decisions… you made without even realizing their full impact.

That's the unseen power of decision-making.

Because even the smallest choice, like the choice to stay comfortable or to step into the unknown, can set off a chain reaction that changes everything.

So, if you want to create a different future, if you want to achieve something bigger, **it all starts with one thing:**

A decision.

In my case, I made my decision.

It was at a time when I was looking at just continuing the same boring, stressful life I had or choosing to make a risky decision that would in fact change my life forever.

It wasn't just something I wanted, it was something I needed to **fulfill my purpose to help others.**

I had to make it happen.

I had no backup plan.

I had to succeed because failure simply wasn't an option for me.

Success meant being able to provide for my family.

It meant fulfilling my dream of finding my place in the world and helping others.

But, you know what happened the moment I made that decision!

Things got worse.

Life tested me.

It hit me harder than ever before.

It felt like the second I made my choice, the universe threw every possible challenge at me to see if I really meant it.

But I held on.

I kept going.

I stuck to my decision with everything I had.

And eventually, I made it happen.

But as you just read, my success was not immediate.

Things didn't magically fall into place.

And that's how life is.

When you decide on something.

When you truly decide.

When you commit to breaking free and creating a better life.

Life doesn't just hand it to you.

It tests your resolve.

It's as if it makes you **prove how much you really want it.**

When you decide to improve, grow, or reach a goal or dream, when you truly decide and start working toward it, you're stepping into the adventure of your life.

You're walking into uncharted territory, breaking free from where you are, reaching for something bigger.

And the moment you do, you'll hit resistance.

Because there's always a barrier between where you are and **where you want to be.**

A kind of ceiling you have to bust through.

A level of discomfort, challenge, and uncertainty you have to overcome.

You'll face setbacks you've never faced before, obstacles that weren't there before, and doubts that try to pull you back to where it's safe, **where it's comfortable.**

And what you have to remember is this:

All of this is simply part of the journey.

It's not a sign to stop.

It's not a sign to turn back.

It's proof that you're moving in the right direction.

Because if you hold on—if you keep pushing through the resistance, the fear, the doubt, and the moments where you question everything—**you will make it.**

And that's where transformation happens.

That's when everything changes.

That's where success begins.

But remember, it all starts with a… **DECISION.**

A real decision.

One made with intention.

Now…

Let's be real.

When you make a big decision, one of those decisions that has the power to change your life, **something shifts.**

You can feel it.

It's like flipping a switch.

If that decision is strong enough, if it's rooted in true conviction, if it's based on a true and strong purpose, if it's something you need as opposed to something that *"would be nice,"* **a sequence of events begins to unfold.**

It's not magic.

It's not luck.

It's the reality of transformation.

And based on my experience, along with countless others, who have achieved success, there's a process.

A pattern.

A series of steps that take place automatically.

You begin to see the world differently.

Opportunities that once seemed invisible start appearing, and your thoughts and actions align with where you want to go rather than where you've been.

You might feel excitement, anticipation, or even fear and doubt.

Emotions rise, because you're stepping into something new, something bigger.

Then, life moves—sometimes aligning in your favor, sometimes falling apart to make space for what's next.

And right when you start making progress, resistance shows up.

Old habits creep back in, doubts whisper in your mind, and even people around you may question your choices.

It's not a sign to stop; it's a sign to keep going.

As you push through, you adapt.

What once felt impossible becomes normal.

You gain confidence, skills, and resilience.

Then, the wins start coming—small at first, then bigger and bigger.

Momentum builds, and before you know it, you've leveled up.

You look back and realize—you're no longer the same person.

It's not always easy, and it's never instant, but if you trust the process and keep moving forward, one decision at a time, **everything changes.**

Looking back on my journey, I can see every moment where this played out.

The decision I made and everything that followed it.

When I made the decision to change my life, I had no idea what was coming.

I just knew I had to keep going.

And that's exactly what I want for you.

But you don't have to do it blindly like I did.

There's a framework, a clear path to follow once you make the decision.

Something that I figured out.

A sort of simple system that will carry you through the process of breaking free and reaching new heights.

Chapter 8:
The Decision Formula

Awareness

Before the decision formula can even begin, there's a crucial moment I call step zero, or ground zero. It's the step that happens before the first step:

Awareness.

This is what happens **before change begins.**

The moment you become aware that something needs to change.

Because, before you ever make a decision.

Before you set a goal of some kind.

You're in a phase of **unawareness.**

You might feel stuck, dissatisfied, or restless, but you haven't fully acknowledged what's really going on. You haven't come to terms with your situation, fully. You haven't really faced what's going on.

Before you can even decide, you first must observe your life without filters, without excuses, without explanations.

See your life as it truly is.

Maybe you have a faint recognition that something's off, that life isn't unfolding the way you hoped.

But you haven't stepped back to take in the full picture.

Maybe you don't know what needs to change.

Maybe you tell yourself you're fine.

Maybe you rationalize why things are the way they are.

Or maybe, deep down, you're not sure change is even possible.

At this stage, things may feel distant, like something you'll deal with "someday."

But then something happens.

A conversation, a wake-up call, a rock-bottom moment, or simply a growing sense that **you're meant for more.**

That's when you shift from **just existing** to **contemplating change.**

This is the moment where a decision becomes possible.

Decide

Everything starts with **a real decision**.

Not a half-hearted wish, not a vague hope, **but true decision.**

A firm commitment.

The kind of decision where there's no turning back.

This is the moment when you say:

"This is it. I'm done staying where I am. I'm ready to change."

But here's the catch:

Deciding to change means **something has to change.**

You can't get a different result by doing the same thing.

That means something in your life needs to shift.

Maybe, you need to leave a toxic relationship.

Maybe, you need to quit a job that's draining you.

Maybe, you need to start that business, invest in yourself, or cut out distractions that are keeping you stuck.

Maybe, you need to take a course to learn a new skill you need to make the change.

Maybe, you're on the right path and you just need a mentor who can provide motivation and inspiration to keep going no matter what.

Change can be uncomfortable—but so is *staying the same*.

And once you decide, you have to follow through.

Because a decision without action is just a wish.

Act

Once you decide, **you have to take action.**

Even if you don't feel ready.

Even if you don't have it all figured out.

Even if it seems scary.

If you are going to change your life, you have to ACT.

This is where most people get stuck.

They make a decision, but they hesitate to take the first step.

They look at what it would take to make it happen, and many give up before even starting.

They overthink.

They wait for the "perfect moment."

But let me tell you what I've learned, the hard way:

There is no perfect moment.

Waiting for the right time is just **fear disguised as logic**.

The only way forward is through action.

Sometimes imperfect.

Sometimes messy.

Sometimes uncomfortable

But always action.

Send that text.

Make that phone call.

Apply for that job.

Start that business.

Post that content.

Show up and take action.

It doesn't have to be perfect.

It just has to be done.

Because **action creates momentum,** and momentum is what keeps you moving forward.

Persist

This is the point where most people quit.

As soon as you start moving, **you will hit resistance.**

Life will test you.

Obstacles will appear out of nowhere.

Not because you're failing—**but because you're growing.**

Remember that **barrier** I talked about?

That ceiling that separates where you are, from where you want to be?

This is where you hit it.

It's the voice in your head that tells you to turn back.

It's the setback that makes you question if you made the right choice.

It's the unexpected challenge that makes you think,

"Maybe this isn't for me."

Remember—**This is normal.**

It happens to everyone.

And the only way to break through is to keep going.

Persist.

Push through the self-doubt.

Push through the discomfort.

Push through the moments where you just want to quit.

Because here is the secret to all this.

If you keep going… you will break through.

Learn

Now, here's something many people don't realize:

Success isn't just about overcoming obstacles.

It's about learning from them.

It's not just about pushing forward.

It's about getting smarter.

Every setback.

Every failure.

Every challenge.

It's teaching you something.

It's not just making you more resilient or "hardened."

You have to ask yourself, ***"What did I learn from this?"***

When you look at successful people, they all have one thing in common:

They learned.

They adapted.

They grew stronger and more confident.

You'll hear them say things like,

"When I look back, I don't even recognize the person I was a year ago."

That's because transformation happens along the way.

Obstacles, challenges, setbacks, and even failure are inevitable.

Don't view them as a road block, as a reason to quit.

See them as necessary lessons on your path to reaching your dream.

When you run into them, in addition to overcoming them, ask yourself.

"What is this challenge teaching me?"

"What actions do I need to take to avoid this in the future?"

"What can I do differently next time?"

The more you learn, the more you evolve.

The smarter and stronger you get.

When you run into those same challenges in the future, you can easily beat them because you already know what to do.

You've been there before.

At first, this process can feel slow, like you're laying the groundwork, figuring things out, and pushing through the struggle.

But somewhere along the line, something shifts.

You've gained enough experience, you've gotten smart enough, you've built momentum, and suddenly, everything starts accelerating.

What once felt impossible now feels natural.

What once took years now happens in months.

And before you know it, you're not just growing—you're soaring.

Celebrate

Alright.

This is the step most people skip.

They work.

They grind.

They push forward… But they never take a moment to breathe, recognize and celebrate how far they've come.

So, here's a simple yet very important part of making your decisions:

Celebrate your wins.

No matter how small or big.

Celebration is essential.

Why?

Because it feeds your **momentum.**

It helps you reset, refocus, and rededicate.

Think of it like this:

Every milestone, every small victory, is a **boost of energy** that propels you to the next level.

Your first day at the gym? **Celebrate.**

Fixed a broken relationship? **Celebrate.**

Got that job you applied for? **Celebrate.**

Got a bonus. **Celebrate.**

Your first sale, your first breakthrough, your first step out of your comfort zone? **Celebrate.**

And it has to be intentional, and it has to be appropriate to the success.

Because when you celebrate, you acknowledge your progress.

You reinforce your ability to make it.

You stay motivated to keep going.

If you don't celebrate?

You burn out.

You start feeling like nothing is ever enough.

You drain your energy.

And pretty soon, you give up and lose hope.

And that's how people lose momentum.

So, take a moment.

Recognize your wins.

Make the journey just as rewarding as the destination.

Yes, there will be challenges.

Yes, there will be setbacks.

But it doesn't have to be all struggle and sacrifice.

Success isn't just about hard work.

It's also about growing, experiencing, and enjoying the adventure.

Celebrate your progress.

Find joy in the small wins.

Laugh along the way.

Make it fun, make it exciting, and embrace every step of the process.

Because the more you enjoy the process, the more unstoppable you become.

And that's how real success happens.

Decide

Now, this last step was the **biggest discovery** I made when figuring out the formula behind making decisions and achieving them.

See, the decision formula is **not a straight path.**

It's not a linear formula that takes you from where you are to where you want to be.

Because your journey doesn't stop at one milestone, one success, or one decision.

Instead, it's a **circle.**

A circle that takes you right back to where you started:

Making a decision.

A new decision.

Whether it's setting your next milestone on the path to your ultimate vision, choosing your next target, or deciding on the next direction to take.

And, even when you finally achieve the dream you've been chasing, the question always comes:

"What's next?"

What's your next adventure?

Your next goal?

Your next dream?

And, big or small, every new step **starts with a decision.**

And that's what keeps the cycle of growth and success moving forward.

And so, the decision formula is in fact a series of decisions, a series of **concentric circles**, each one expanding outward.

One decision leads to the next, then the next, and then the next, creating a cycle of continuous expansion.

Each new decision propelling you to higher levels of success.

It's a continuous journey of progress, momentum, and evolution.

The Decision Formula Diagram

When I made my first million, I was faced with a new reality.

I had done what I set out to do.

And immediately after I celebrated, I was faced with a decision.

Was I going to sit back and stay where I was?

Was I going to settle?

Or was I going to decide again—push forward, aim higher, and take everything I had learned to the next level?

I'll be honest. I chose to settle.

I made my first million, and I coasted for a few years making a million dollars per year.

I had not figured out this whole decision making process yet. But I finally did realize that the truth is you should never really settle. You need to make new decisions to keep growing. There is no successful coasting in life for the long term.

And remember, this **decide** step isn't just for when you've reached your ultimate goal, it applies to every milestone, every achievement, big or small, along the way.

Let's look at how this plays out in real life.

Imagine someone who's single and decides:

I want to find someone who truly loves me, and whom I truly love.

They go out, meet people, and eventually, they find that special person.

They celebrate this moment—because finding real love isn't always easy.

But now what?

A new decision is needed.

Maybe that decision is to deepen the relationship, to commit to something bigger.

They decide to get engaged.

Then they get married.

Another milestone.

Another celebration.

They've found their partner for life.

But after the honeymoon, after the excitement, what comes next?

A new decision.

To stay committed.

To build a life together.

To navigate the ups and downs, not just when things are easy, but when challenges come.

And years later, maybe they hit a rough patch.

Ten years in, things aren't as smooth as they used to be.

Stress, life, and responsibilities have piled up.

The connection feels strained.

But instead of giving up, they make a new decision:

To fight for their marriage.

To fix what's broken.

To stay together, not just because they said "I do" a decade ago, but because they are choosing—again— to be with each other.

They work through it.

They rebuild.

And when they come out stronger, they celebrate again.

But after that?

Another decision.

To keep growing together.

To never stop working on their relationship.

To make sure love doesn't become stagnant, but instead, evolves into something even deeper.

This is the cycle of life.

And it applies to anything you decide to achieve or do.

Decide.

Act.

Persist.

Learn.

Celebrate.

And then… decide again.

At every stage, you're faced with a new choice.

You don't stop.

You don't "arrive" and stay there forever.

You keep deciding.

You keep climbing and you keep your dreams alive and growing.

Because **life doesn't stand still, and neither should you.**

So, whatever stage you're in, whether you're just beginning, in the thick of it, or celebrating a win, keep this in mind:

Your next breakthrough is just one decision away.

And that's the exact formula, and if you follow it, you will achieve your goals, and you will grow, expand, and level up to a life you never thought possible.

And all of it starts with a decision!

But there's one more thing you need to know.

The Untold Secret about Decisions

Now, you may have noticed something in my story.

When I made that decision, it stuck.

I didn't waver.

I didn't fall back into old patterns.

Somehow, that one decision carried me through thick and thin, through obstacles, doubts, and challenges.

And at some point, I had to ask myself:

Why?

This wasn't the first time I had decided to live a better life.

It wasn't the first time I told myself I was ready for change.

But what was different this time?

Why did this decision stick while so many others faded?

I sat with that question.

I thought back on all the times I had made commitments to change, only to abandon them weeks, or even days later.

And that's when I uncovered **something huge.**

A **major secret** about decisions.

The difference between the ones that transform your life and the ones that disappear like a passing thought.

See, we make decisions **every single day.**

Some big.

Some small.

But let's be honest, how many of those decisions actually stick?

Think about it.

How many times have you decided to go after a goal... only to let it slip away, because life got too busy, obstacles piled up, or the excitement faded?

How many times have you told yourself *"this time will be different"*—only to fall back into old habits when things got tough?

How many times have you started with energy and motivation, only to watch your commitment slowly disappear, replaced by excuses, distractions, or self-doubt?

Why does this happen?

How do you make a decision that actually lasts?

What makes the difference?

What separates a real, life-changing decision from just another good intention?

Well, I took a step back and looked at my own journey.

I reflected on the moments when I made decisions that truly changed everything, and the times when I made decisions that slowly faded into the background.

Then, I looked at others.

People who had built success, who had transformed their lives, who had broken through barriers and never looked back.

And that's when I saw it.

The single biggest difference.

The secret to why some decisions stick, fueling unstoppable momentum and lasting change, while others disappear like a passing thought.

And here's the secret:

**For a decision to be unstoppable
it has to be fueled by a true purpose
and it has to be bigger than you.**

When I made my decision to become a millionaire, it wasn't just about me.

Yes, I wanted financial freedom.

Yes, I wanted success.

But what really drove me?

What powered my persistence through countless setbacks and reasons to give up?

I wanted to help thousands of others achieve success too.

I had a family to take care of.

I had people counting on me.

And behind it all, I had a purpose bigger than myself.

A purpose I had been searching for my whole life.

And **that's** what gave me the strength to push through every obstacle, setback, and challenge that came my way.

Because when your decision **aligns with your true purpose** and is **bigger than yourself**, giving up is no longer an option.

There's a difference between decisions made out of simple desire and those driven by something deeper.

Many choices are made with good intentions, plans to improve, work harder, or chase a goal simply because it seems like a good idea at the time.

But without a stronger foundation, those decisions often fade.

Now, compare that with the moments in life, when following through wasn't optional.

The times, when circumstances demanded action, when others were depending on it, when the stakes were too high to walk away.

In those moments, the decision wasn't just about what was *wanted*—it was about what was *necessary*.

And that changes everything.

That's the key.

When your decision is tied to something **bigger than just your own comfort**, something deeper, whether it's your family, your **true purpose**, your future, or even a deep personal conviction, you tap into a level of commitment that **nothing can shake.**

Because when quitting means letting down the people you love…

When stopping means going back to a life you refuse to accept…

When giving up means staying stuck in a version of yourself you've outgrown…

You keep going.

You push through the hard days.

You fight through the setbacks.

You do whatever it takes, not because it's easy, but because **it's necessary.**

That's the difference between a weak decision and a strong one.

A weak decision is based on **desire.**

A strong decision is based on **purpose.**

And purpose is what carries you through, when motivation fades, when life gets hard, when doubt creeps in.

And that's when everything changes.

Because here is the truth:

You are capable of achieving your dreams.

Yes—**YOU.**

I know that, because I've been where you are.

I've had doubts.

I've faced setbacks.

I've wondered if success was even possible for me.

And here's what I realized:

The only difference between those who succeed and those who don't is that those who succeed <u>believe they can and know they will.</u>

Look at any successful person, and you'll see their achievements.

But what you won't see are all the barriers they had to overcome to get there.

The sheer persistence, dedication, and resilience that carried them through every obstacle, every challenge, and every moment when quitting felt easier than continuing.

And guess what?

You have that same power inside you.

I truly believe you are far more capable than you've been led to believe.

And I want you to believe that, too.

Because that dream, that goal, that vision you have for your life?

Whatever it is—IT IS POSSIBLE!

You don't need permission.

You don't need to wait for the perfect time.

You don't need to have it all figured out.

You don't need a perfect plan or fail-proof idea.

You don't need to be born into privilege or have all the answers right now.

What you need is the **Belief** that **You Can Do This.**

And the Certainty that you will.

Because here is the undeniable truth.

YOU CAN!

Your Journey to Success

If you've made it this far, then I know something about you.

You're not just here to wish about success.

You're here, because something inside you knows you are meant for more.

Something inside you is pushing for more.

More growth. More success. More freedom.

And there's something inside you that tells you you can make it.

And even if doubt creeps in, even if you're not 100% sure of yourself or your decision, there's still a part of you that **believes it's possible.**

Maybe you're looking for a better way to achieve your dreams.

Maybe you just need guidance, support, or the right strategy.

That's why I created **The Millionaire's Club.**

This isn't just another course, just another program, or just another motivational talk.

This isn't about hype.

It's not about empty motivation or feel-good inspiration that fades once you hit the reality of getting started.

The Millionaire's Club is a community.

A mentorship.

A real blueprint for success.

I've taken everything I've learned, the exact steps, the formulas, the mindset shifts, the strategies that took me from massive debt and anxiety to a happy and fulfilled millionaire.

I've put them into a system that you can follow, step by step.

And inside The Millionaire's Club, I'm not just giving you information.

I provide education, motivation, and the inspiration that keeps you moving forward—**even when things get tough.**

This is where we work together to make sure your dreams don't fade away. Where we apply the principles that build real success. Where you get a chance to not just dream, but to actually make it happen.

And I want you to be a part of it, because here's the truth:

True success isn't a solo journey.

The people around you shape the way you think, the decisions you make, and ultimately, the results you achieve. They can either lift you higher or hold you back.

The Millionaire's Club is about surrounding yourself with driven, success-minded individuals, people who not only want to win but also want to see you win.

You don't have to do this alone. With the right knowledge, the right strategies, and the right people in your corner, **anything is possible.**

So, make the decision. Not just to dream about success, but to start **building it.** This could be the decision that changes everything.

I'll see you inside.

Love,
Jim

For more information on
The Millionaires Club
visit www.jimmathers.com
or scan the below QR code: